TRUST BASED

Time Management & Productivity

Proven Ways to Stop Dawdling and Start Achieving

MARK GIVEN

Founder of the Trust Based Philosophy™

For publishing consideration:
markgivenseminars@gmail.com

ISBN:
Hardcover — 978-1-7320146-2-6
Paperback — 978-1-7320146-9-5
Ebook—

WHAT OTHERS ARE SAYING...

"Having known Mark Given for 20 years, I know he lives his philosophy of *TRUST* Based Leadership, Sales and Success every day. He has shared that knowledge with you in this book."

Zan Monroe, CEO, Author, Speaker & Coach, Motivator

"There are writers and speakers and then there are teachers. My good friend Mark is a teacher. He has captured the essence of the most critical aspect of relationships in a way that made me reflect on my own life and leadership. This short read has long-term impact. Thank you Mark for compiling such profound information on a *Trust Based Philosophy*."

Jackie Leavenworth, Author, International Speaker, Trainer and Business Coach

"My friend, Mark Given has created his life and business based on building *Trust*. Now you have an amazing opportunity to learn his Trust Based Philosophy. Read his book.....it can change your life!"

Jo Mangum, Coach, VP of Training-Century21, Author of The Strategic Agent®

"Mark lives his life by the values he shares about *Trust*. This book will not only show you how to build *Trust*, but how to use it and apply the principles in your everyday life. This book is a must read!"

Lee Barrett, Author, Tutor, National Real Estate Instructor, Company President

"I've not only had the privilege of seeing Mark teach but also taught alongside him so I know firsthand that as a teacher and author his message is engaging... genuine ... and, impactful! If you have not yet had the "Mark experience" this is a must read."

Ed Hatch, International NLP Trainer,
Author, Coach – Master Negotiator

"Having worked with Mark in business and volunteer situations, he has my complete *Trust*. His books share discoveries and techniques that are easy to understand and implement immediately."

Pat Zaby, REALTOR® and Highly Respected
National Speaker and Teacher

"*Trust* Mark to create strategies that can be immediately implemented by everyone!"

Frank Serio, Past National President–
Council of Residential Specialists

"Mark has provided for us an excellent resource to apply what we know is needful for *Trust*. I love his list of concepts to make ourselves more trustworthy. The beauty in this book is in asking yourself the questions he provides and adding thoughtful answers to lock the concept into your regular practice of leading."

Monica Neubauer, Speaker, Podcaster

"Mark is a Master Teacher and his Trust Based Philosophy has the power to improve lives and businesses."

Larry Kendall, Author of Ninja Selling, Deep Thinker,
Industry Changer

"We believe one of Mark's paramount aims is to help build a better YOU; he uses the principles of TRUST to do that. Grab one of his books and sit down for a fun read. Guaranteed you will learn some valuable information."

Jason Donahey, National Director of
Sales Patch Rubber Company

Katrina Donahey, LPN and Caretaker

"Thank you Mark for an easy and informative read! This is a book that anyone can read and then apply the principles to life and/or business. Sure, you can have some success without TRUST, but is that really the best way? Mark lays out a methodology for gaining true TRUST with anyone you encounter. TRUST is earned and so is SUCCESS. I highly recommend Mark's book!"

Heather Platz, Experienced Executive Assistant and
Master Sales Agent

"Mark has a way to make his point in a fun, quick and non-judge-y way. I love him as a brother and mentor! This easy-to-read book will set you on the right track!"

John C Stark, Managing Broker
Coldwell Banker Des Moines, IA

"As usual, Mark Given delivers. Easy to read, understandable and ideas I can (& will) use. I recommend this book to everyone who wants to "be better."

Marian Goetzinger, Owner Pine Knoll Shores Realty, Inc

"Mark Given is the new Dale Carnegie!"

Pam Hargrave, Multi-Million Dollar Sales Producer for over 20 years

"Mark has been immersed in and committed to sharing positive life-altering strategies in his ***Trust Based Philosophy*** series of books. Content-rich, easy to absorb, thought provoking and result-oriented, actionable principles anyone can apply. This is a must-read and I highly recommend it."

Robert Morris, President Middle Tennessee AOR/ National Speaker & Teacher

Speaking and Teaching Testimonials and Endorsements

"If you are looking for a speaker, trainer and coach that can empower, inspire, and motivate your group then you must book my friend Mark Given!"

James Malinchak, Featured on ABC's *Secret Millionaire,* Best Selling Author of 20 Books

"I love and trust Mark and I know he can deliver on teaching your organization how to achieve more success by following his Trust Based Philosophy."

Jack Canfield – Co-Creator, #1 NY Times Best-Selling Book Series *Chicken Soup for the Soul*®

"We hire Mark to share his Trust Based Philosophy in leadership, sales and success with our 1500 members every year!"

Zan Monroe, CEO Long Leaf Pine Association, Author, Speaker and Coach

"You are simply an event planners dream! I have been involved with contracting hundreds of speakers for various programs over the last 24+ years and I consider Mark as an exemplary example of an ideal speaker."

Rebecca Fletcher, Director, GIRE – VP of Education

"My reason for inviting you back time and time again is purely selfish…it makes me look good. I thank you for the time you invest in crafting your message to meet our specific needs. I thank you for the energy you pump into our company. And, I thank you for your friendship. You are a class act that is very good at what you do. I look forward to our continued relationship and am anxious to have you back soon!"

Kit Hale, Principal Broker/
Managing Partner MKB, REALTORS

"Creating and nurturing a successful business without trust, is not possible. Being a leader without trust, is not possible. In fact, having fantastic relationships without trust, is not possible. Learning about and cultivating methods of developing trust then, must come from a source that is trustworthy. Mark Given is just that source. A colleague and friend for over 16 years, I can't imagine anyone more qualified to take YOU on the trust journey."

Rich Sands, Head Honcho, Rich Sands Seminars

DEDICATION

It is with profound admiration, respect and love that I dedicate this book and all that I do personally and professionally to my wonderful wife Janice (Gigi), our sons Blaine, Chase, Kyle, and Taylor, our daughter Kerri, our daughters-in-law Janelle, Bonnie, Lauren, and Gabbie and our son-in law Dylan, as well as our growing crop of beautiful and gifted grandchildren (now 8 and growing). Without them, my life and work would be incomplete, and I would not know the JOY I have experienced nearly every day of my life. Through the years, I have learned and grown because of many master teachers and speakers that have inspired me. Some know who they are, and some do not, but nonetheless, I thank each of you (there is a list at the back of this book).

Gigi is my greatest and most positive guide on this earth, but without reservation, I thank my Heavenly Father and His Son, Jesus Christ; without them, none of the positive events or decisions I have ever experienced in my life would have been possible. THEY have proven over and over to me that nearly everything good is possible with <u>Focus</u> and <u>Determination</u> followed by <u>ACTION</u>!

A MESSAGE TO YOU FROM MARK...

Every day, *just like you*, each of us strives to be our best and focus on making a positive difference in this wonderful world.

You want to SUCCEED, help your family, be a good friend, make a secure living and be remembered as someone that can be counted on and **_trusted_**. I want that too*!*

You already know that building or maintaining **Trust** is a top priority for people that are striving to create a life of significance (and that sounds just like YOU too).

Trusting in yourself and with those with whom you surround yourself is a critical link to all good relationships whether personal or professional.

Trust is a primary principle in how people work together effectively, build deep and powerful relationships, and listen to one another.

Lack of **Trust** creates poor PRODUCTIVITY, low energy, and reduced SUCCESS.

So...in this important book, you WILL learn how to build **Trust** in many ways and do it more often as you focus on **TIME MANAGEMENT & PRODUCTIVITY**.

You will learn how to lead by example, communicate more openly, take responsible action, and create more personal success by improving your **TIME MANAGEMENT & PRODUCTIVITY** skills.

Read this book. Then…share it with a friend. They **Trust** in YOU and in your opinion.

And…thank-you for taking the time to INVEST IN YOURSELF AND IN YOUR FUTURE! You never lose when you are striving to learn how to better maximize your **TIME MANAGEMENT & PRODUCTIVITY** skills!

CONTENTS

INTRODUCTION

Mark Given Interviewed by Kevin Harrington

Original Shark on ABC's Hit TV Show "Shark
Tank" and Inventor of the Infomercial

Kevin: Hi! I'm Kevin Harrington, an original shark from the hit ABC TV show **Shark Tank** and I'm here with Mark Given. Mark is Founder of the Trust Based Philosophy and Trust Based Academy. He is a speaker and Amazon #1 Best-Selling Author and goes all around the country speaking about the Trust Based Philosophy. Mark, I want to say thanks for being here.

Mark: Thank-you Kevin...It's my pleasure!

Kevin: We go back a number of years Mark. In fact, I have endorsed your books. It is immensely powerful what you're doing and getting so many speaking engagements is proof that what you're doing is landing in the marketplace. So, tell me how you got started with the Trust Based Philosophy.

Mark: Sure Kevin. My whole life has been about trying to be a trustworthy person and I realized that there is a science behind Trust, it's not just a concept.

Kevin: Right

Mark: So, some 40 years ago, I started studying it, trying to understand the science behind building, repairing, and maintaining trust. I was interested in how to create it and then how to fix it when there is a problem.

Kevin: Okay…Does this work with husbands and wives too?

Mark: It does!

Kevin: Across the board?

Mark: Kevin, it works for companies and organizations, associations, educators, physicians, lawyers, and every profession you could think of, but most of all…it works for PEOPLE!

Kevin: So…you might keep some families together?

Mark: That's right, and companies and industries too. You know trust is such an important principle because our whole life and business begins when we establish trust and it crushes, it crumbles, it just all comes apart when we destroy trust.

Kevin: Yes…I certainly agree with that.

Mark: So, I spend my life trying to help people understand not just what trust is, but how to improve it and direct it…How to create, nurture and repair TRUST.

Kevin: I love it!

Mark: And how to make trust deeper and better.

Kevin: So, people out there who may be listening to our interview or reading the transcript, they may be saying I think I already have some levels of trust, but it may not be powerful enough, deep enough or it may not be what they think trust actually is either, right? So, it has got to be a mutual situation between people, right?

Mark: Of course...and as I travel and speak to organizations, associations and groups all over whether it be education or corporate, I actually teach them our Four Facets of Trust which is something they have never heard or even known about.

Kevin: Right.

Mark: Kevin, we all know that we only get one opportunity to make a first impression.

Kevin: Right

Mark: I teach people how to have a much better, more successful opening and then we teach the rapport building FACET which is...

Kevin: You only get one chance to make a good impression.

Mark: Exactly...but we're not taught the best way to do that. We've all been taught that first impressions are important but not exactly how to create our BEST first impression. I teach people how to do that.

Kevin: Right

Mark: I then teach the Rapport Building FACET which is all about learning to ask more questions and better questions and then really listen.

Kevin: Okay

Mark: And so you learn to probe in a really good, interesting, sincere, and transparent way. After the Rapport FACET, I follow with the Maintenance FACET.

Kevin: Okay

Mark: The Maintenance FACET is all about how to maintain trust over a long period of time.

Kevin: Right, that makes sense.

Mark: And then I teach the Repair FACET. This FACET is about the science and steps of a proper apology and how when we mess up, the proper steps to fixing it. We are all make mistakes. Repair is critical.

Kevin: Yes, I love it. Now you currently have 4 different versions of Trust book.

Mark: I do.

Kevin: You have *Trust Based Success*. You also have *Trust Based Selling* for sales people…I mean I've always been a Zig Ziglar fan, and he was a big guy in this regard.

Mark: Yes …Zig sure was.

Kevin: *Trust Based Networking*. This book hits home with the direct selling world out there and I bet many other industries, and what's the fourth?

Mark: *Trust Based Leadership*

Kevin: *Trust Based Leadership* is not just for corporate clients…is it? You're very passionate about all this Mark, and I can just feel it sitting here and I love getting together with you. How come this has become your primary focus? Was there a point where you had some bad experience about trust or how did you develop this whole concept and these important principles?

Mark:　That's a great question Kevin. After college, I started my own company. I grew that retail company for about 20 years until I sold it.

Kevin:　Okay, took some chips off the table.

Mark:　That's right. I started with one little location and ended up with 47.

Kevin:　Okay

Mark:　As an example, one thing I learned was that if my people did not trust me, they would not embrace my vision. Instead, they would only focus on their own vision.

Kevin:　Right.

Mark:　I learned that our customers and clients, if they didn't trust us, then they didn't come back. It was one and done and we needed them to come back to do more business with us and we needed them to send us repeat and referral business, to recommend us to other people. We needed them to be our advocates. So, I really started studying trust as a result of wanting and needing my business to succeed. And in addition, I wanted my marriage and my life to be happy and full.

Kevin:　Right

Mark:　What I discovered is that most of the books out there are just on the concept of trust, but not the science of trust and not how to actually be better at it.

Kevin: I gotcha

Mark: So, I started going to work trying to figure it out and as a result have written these books and I have more books coming out in the Trust Based Philosophy series.

Kevin: Love it.

Mark: It's an ongoing thing. I actually think I'll do it to study and write about this until I die.

Kevin: There you go. Well you know it's a four-step process and my mind is going right towards the repair side because I'm thinking somebody knows they have a problem, you're a problem solver, right? You can teach people how to start from the opening relationship but sometimes people may come to you because they've had the issue where they need repair.

Mark: Sure, but I also teach the pro-active side. How to be better at building and maintaining trust.

Kevin: So, does it start at any one of those points, or at times is the repair principle where people really need you right now.

Mark: Actually, I have companies, organizations, associations, leadership and sales teams, colleges and people that will call me or email me and say here's our problem...we need your help. Can you come and speak to our group or at our event and teach us how to do a better job of building trust to increase our success?

Kevin: Right

Mark: Companies have called me before and said, "Hey Mark, we messed up. What are the proper steps for us to improve this? What should we be thinking about? We don't know what we don't know so help us know what we need to know."

Kevin: Gotcha

Mark: What I do is teach people, companies, and organizations the steps to a proper apology. Kevin, we all know how interesting social media is today. Everybody seems to have an opinion and many feel the need to share it anonymously! It used to be that if you upset one person, they might tell 100. Now you can upset one person and they tell hundreds of thousands of people, right?

Kevin: Right

Mark: We try and help individuals or a company or organization or associations understand that there is a science and a proper way to apologize. You cannot force people to accept your apology though…and…we need others to recognize that we are not always perfect, and that when we're not, we're interested and sincere about fixing it.

Kevin: Right

Mark: But to repair, to rebuild trust, you have got to go through the proper steps to do that.

Kevin: Right

Mark: There really is a science to achieving that.

Kevin: Love it. I always love to find the unique aspect of what you're doing over others and I think you've just said it. You address the science of trust and not just the concept of trust.

Mark: Kevin, that is absolutely correct!

Kevin: Whereas others just talk about it, you've uncovered the 4 steps to building and maintaining trust and the science to repairing it at the very end if that's needed. What are the biggest challenges that companies are having in this world now? I mean, you talk about social media and the difference today vs. say ten years ago, how do people deal with these challenges that are out there in your world of trust?

Mark: Leadership is obviously a critical point in the process of repairing because what you do is way more powerful than what people just see. Media and marketing can help drive positive or negative attention but the truth is what you actually do and promote that will ultimately create society's true perception. So, authenticity is what I'm saying here. We teach a lot about what's your authentic position, what is it you're really trying to do in the world.

Kevin: Right

Mark: You may create a product but that is just what you sell. What's the culture and the systems behind that product so people will want to do business with you. People just have the ability now to research anything, so companies need to be more authentic about their purpose. They need to be more transparent just like individuals need to be more transparent. Kevin, people today can see right through us.

Kevin: Yes, yes.

Mark: It doesn't take long at all for people to see the real you.

Kevin: That is right. Fantastic! There are people out there – direct selling people, entrepreneurs, executives that can benefit from one of these trust books that you've written, but are there some words of encouragement to those that are out there right now, and maybe how they might be able to reach you or contact you? Let's try and help those that are here right now. Give some words of encouragement on the whole business of trust.

Mark: Sure Kevin. Obviously, I've tried very hard to make it easy for people to find me. We are actually creating a new program called the Trust Based Academy, so you'll be able to find us that way also. But just click on **www.markgiven.com.** It's easy to find me there, or, if they just look up trust, hopefully we've got the right triggers out there for them to find something that links back to me. On my website, there is plenty of information about what we do and how to reach me and they can even sign up for my FREE weekly Mark's Minute.

Kevin: Okay so you have some free downloads and some free information.

Mark: Yes, we do!

Kevin: That is great Mark. When I think of today's world and how much we need what you teach. Trust and Authenticity…excellent! You know I've been in the business of selling products direct to the consumer for almost 40 years. In the old days, it was hard sell. Today, the world and especially millennials don't want that hard sell. They want a trust-based relationship. They want authenticity and I think it's great to see that you're filling their needs at this point. Thanks for being here today Mark, and I just want to say people should have all four of these books.

Mark: You bet!

Kevin: We've got Mark Given here and we've been talking about the Trust Based Philosophy. Mark's written four books of trust so far with more to come. You've got to go to his website **www.MarkGiven.com** and check it all out. This is really exciting. Mark, thanks for being here.

Mark: Thank you Kevin, it's absolutely been a pleasure my friend!

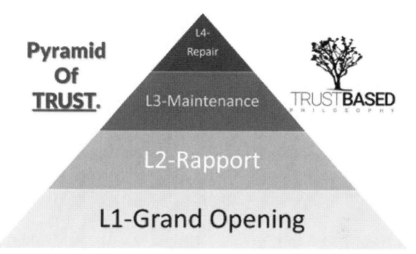

Pyramid Of TRUST.

- L4-Repair
- L3-Maintenance
- L2-Rapport
- L1-Grand Opening

TRUST**BASED**
PHILOSOPHY

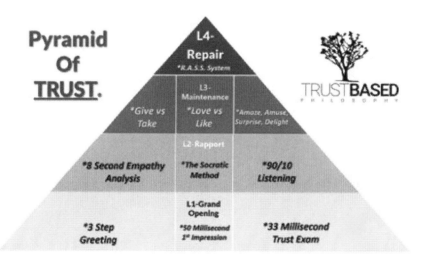

Pyramid Of TRUST.

TRUST**BASED**
PHILOSOPHY

	L4-Repair *R.A.S.S. System	
*Give vs Take	L3-Maintenance *Love vs Like	*Amaze, Amuse, Surprise, Delight
*8 Second Empathy Analysis	L2-Rapport *The Socratic Method	*90/10 Listening
*3 Step Greeting	L1-Grand Opening *50 Millisecond 1st Impression	*33 Millisecond Trust Exam

TRUST BASED
PHILOSOPHY

TRUST BASED
ACADEMY

TRUST BASED
COACHING

THE ORIGIN OF TIME MANAGEMENT

Time management...you know what it is and whether you control it, or it controls you...

There are some experts that say Time Management originated in Denmark as a training device to help busy executives organize their time more effectively.

Other researchers have refuted those thoughts and provided evidence that the earliest references to Time Management come from Benedictine monks. These focused and determined monks lived around the sixth century AD and there is some proof that they made a consistent point of scheduling their daily activities...of course with positive results.

And yet...there are other scholars that regard Benjamin Franklin as the father of Time Management. Our brother Ben's approach might be summed up with one of his many recognized and frequently referenced quips...

Ben eloquently said...

"If you want to enjoy one of the greatest luxuries in life, the luxury of having enough time, time to rest, time to think things through, time to get things done and know you have done them to the best of your ability, remember there is only one way. Take enough "time" to think and plan things in the order of their importance. Your life will take on a new zest, you will add years to your life and more life to your years. Let all your things have their places."

But…regardless of who actually is the author of Time Management, one fact persists, and we are each affected by understanding and leveraging its importance…

I would simply say…

"No matter where you live, no matter how intelligent or wealthy or important or social you may or may not be…no matter that you are a king or a pauper…there are only 1,440 minutes in a day, 10,080 minutes in a week, 525,600 minutes in a year, and if you're lucky…42,048,000 minutes in your life…it's how you choose to **_invest_** the composite of those minutes that creates a fullness of joy, happiness, contentment, and success!"

"Time is the school in which we learn, time is the fire in which we burn."
—Delmore Schwartz

What are 5 things I can do right now to better invest my next 1,440 minutes?

_____

_____

_____

_____

_____

_____

_____

_____

_____

_____

_____

_____

_____

_____

_____

_____

_____

TRUST BASED
PHILOSOPHY

TRUST BASED
ACADEMY

TRUST BASED
COACHING

TIME MANAGEMENT AND THE PARETO PRINCIPLE

More than likely, you have heard of the Pareto Principle.

The **Pareto** principle (also known as the 80/20 rule, the law of the vital few, or the principle of factor sparsity) suggests that, for many parts of your life and your business, 80% of your results will come from 20% of your activities.

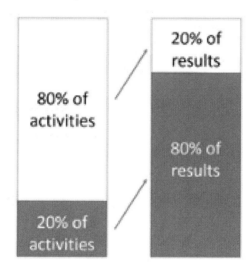

For Alfredo Pareto, his 80/20 principle applied to farming and European wealth.

But now, we realize that the 80/20 rule also applies to shoes, or carpet, or Time Management, or wealth, or sales, or happiness, or...well...you could choose almost anything.

It's an important law of success that cannot be ignored.

So...as the Pareto Principle relates to Time Management and Productivity, you will become more determined to identify and focus on the relatively small 20% of your schedule that actually produces 80% of your success...and...as a result, you will boldly cheer at your improved Productivity.

Here's a couple ways I would suggest you do that:

1. Clearly identify the relatively few things you do (or should be doing) daily that produce quality results.

    a. In business, that should be connecting regularly with your clients on a more personal level–especially on those magical and important days. Prove to them how they are important to you both as a client and as a person.

    b. In marriage, it would be anything that shows your spouse that you love them and are listening to them. For me...it would be regularly cleaning the kitchen without being asked (one of Gigi's least favorite things to do is clean the kitchen).

    c. As a leader, it would be knowing the hire dates, birthdays and anniversaries, names of their spouse and their children, then taking a moment to briefly celebrate with them when those important days come around (and by celebrating I mean that just mentioning that you know and remembered is a huge win).

2. Set a few minutes aside every morning, or every night, or at the end of your workday to focus on the most important tasks for your next day.

    a. Maintaining a simple and visible Today's Priorities list every day can help you be more organized, more focused, and more Productive.

b. A Today's Priorities list is just as effective on a weekend as it is on a weekday, so get in the habit of doing it regularly and repeatedly.

Today's Priorities

1. _____

2. _____

3. _____

4. _____

5. _____

The key to this system is not to check the box after you have completed the task, but rather to randomly write down your priorities as they come to mind...then...place a number in the box to help you with flow. Assuming there are 5 items written, choose which one you should do first...ie...prioritize your 5 items by importance.

This all may sound simple, but the practice is apparently not simplistic because so few people I know actually do it.

And...if you do think that I'm right, you will have to make an investment in time, planning, and consistency to make sure you make it an important part of every day.

Don't be fooled by thinking that it takes a lot of effort to find the time to create your mini list, because it doesn't...and if you've read my series of Trust Based Philosophy books, you might remember that John David Mann wrote in his book *The Slight*

Edge that…*things that are easy to do are also easy not to do*… that's why the average person will never take a couple minutes to write down their daily priorities!

Get to work…YOU'RE NOT AVERAGE, and you will be so glad you created this new habit!

P.S. You will also find that within your 20% is another super 20%…the Best of the Best. Take extra special care to identify the ultimate uses of your time which will help you create the abundance you are seeking.

"It's how we spend our time here and now, that really matters. If you are fed up with the way you have come to interact with time, change it."

—Marcia Wieder

What are 3 of the most productive things you should be doing on a daily basis that will guarantee higher levels of Productivity and help you achieve an abundance of RESULTS?

_____

_____

_____

_____

_____

_____

_____

_____

_____

_____

_____

_____

_____

_____

_____

TRUST BASED
PHILOSOPHY

TRUST BASED
ACADEMY

TRUST BASED
COACHING

TIME MANAGEMENT AND THE COVEY PRINCIPLE

Stephen Covey was a wise man, a brilliant thinker, and a writer that many authors have patterned their entire principles on... and why not...Covey got it (I wish I could have known him personally or been lucky enough to take a couple of classes with him).

You may have never read his book "First Things First", so I thought it would make good sense to share my cliff notes with you. Here's what Stephen taught me.

*Basing our happiness on our ability to control everything in life is futile.

*A meaningful life is more a matter of what you do and why you do it rather than how fast you can get it done.

*Most people relate to the three generations of time management:

a. First Generation – simple notes and checklists

b. Second Generation – calendars and appointment books

c. Third Generation – clarifying your short, medium, and long- term goals – prioritizing on a daily basis

*Covey believed there are 8 Basic Approaches to Time Management:

1. **The Get Organized Approach**–caused by the lack of order in our lives. We often cannot find what we want when we want it…the downside is we spend more time organizing than we do producing.

2. **The Warrior Approach**–caused by a desire to protect our personal time…the downside is we feel others are the enemy.

3. **The ABC or Prioritization Approach**–based on the concept of sequence…the downside is that sometimes this approach brings us what we wanted only to discover that it didn't bring us lasting happiness.

4. **The Goal Approach** – basically says…know what you want and focus your effort to achieve it. Many folks use this to climb the ladder of success only to find that it's leaning against the wrong wall.

5. **The Magic Tool Approach** – always use the right tool, the right software program, the right planner, etc. The downside is there is always a new tool.

6. **The Time Management 101 Approach** – the idea here is that we must master time management. Doing that will bring you more inner peace, richer relationships, or greater satisfaction.

7. **The Go with the Flow Approach** – getting back to the natural rhythm of living will open our lives to spontaneity and serendipity, drawing on Eastern Cultures. The downside is that vital elements like vision, purpose, and balance are frequently missing.

8. **The Recovery Approach**–built on a fear of delegating and a tendency to micromanage. Self-awareness is valuable, but understanding it is only part of creating change.

Ultimately…I believe Stephen's focus in writing the book was to direct us towards considering what's the most important thing we could do this week to have the greatest positive impact… understanding that sometimes we get so busy sawing that we forget to sharpen the saw…and that we should also load our big rocks first.

Wise and prudent advice…don't you agree?

"The key is in not spending time, but in investing it."

—Stephen R. Covey

Of Stephen Covey's 8 Basic Approaches to Time Management, which one freaks you out the most and causes you the most indigestion?

_____

_____

_____

_____

_____

_____

_____

_____

_____

_____

_____

_____

_____

_____

_____

_____

_____

TIME MANAGEMENT AND THE LAW OF PARKINSON

Parkinson's law is defined as... *"work expands so as to fill the time available for its completion"*.

In simpler words, Parkinson believes that the amount of time YOU have to perform a task is equal to the amount of time it takes YOU to complete the task...but...is he right?

In other words, work complicates itself to the point that it fills all the available time allocated to the project...and...work contracts to equal the time given you to finish the task.

So...if that is YOU...what will YOU do?

Here are 6 Surefire Ways to Beat Parkinson's Law:

1. Break Down Your Tasks and Deadlines–Parkinson's Law always strikes the hardest when you have enormous tasks with far-away deadlines and it appears that you have plenty of time to get the task completed with time to spare.

2. Know What "Done" Means – think the job through before you begin the work, so you are more realistic about all the steps necessary to say the job really is "done".

3. Set Clear Boundaries – are you working on more than one project at a time with many tasks... set boundaries on doing the first things first.

4. Challenge Yourself – YOU are not average so act that way. An average person suffers from Parkinson's Law, but not you...not anymore! Take

a realistic look at why you may have been guilty of this problem in the past and stop...now!

5. Create Incentives to Finish Early – most people, just like YOU are goal oriented, so if you were to reward yourself for getting the job done early, you might avoid being a victim of Parkinson's Law. Why not consider rewarding yourself each time you complete something significant on your list of tasks. (give yourself a cookie, ice cream or if you are dieting, broccoli...how about a short break or a fun evening out...you choose).

6. Know What's Next – There is always another project in your immediate future, and sometimes those upcoming projects excite you more than what you are currently working on. Don't let Parkinson's Law slow you down right now preventing you from moving on to that next more exciting project...get these tasks and this job done first so you can start working on that more thrilling project sooner.

(HT – Litemind.com)

No matter how you cut it, many people are a victim of Parkinson's Law...if that's YOU...it's time to STOP!

"Time is the wisest counselor of all."

—Pericles

Are you a victim of Parkinson's Law? What could you do today to be more focused, press forward, and get that job done quicker?

_____

_____

_____

_____

_____

_____

_____

_____

_____

_____

_____

_____

_____

_____

_____

_____

_____

We had a scheduling challenge,
so tomorrow's deadline has been moved to yesterday.

TIME MANAGEMENT AND THE POSEC METHOD

POSEC is an acronym for "Prioritizing by Organizing, Streamlining, Economizing and Contributing."

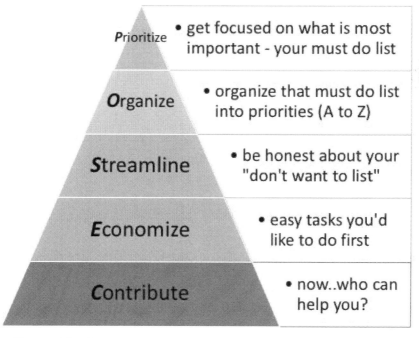

Created by Steven Lam, the POSEC Method is loosely derived from Abraham Maslow's Hierarchy of Needs.

Lam explains in his writings that this method, like Maslow's theory, gives an individual, just like you, a realistic tool for setting priorities as they pertain to your unique needs and your personal life goals.

So how can you utilize the POSEC Method to be more efficient?

1. Use the prioritize step to decide what you really want.

2. Streamlining will automatically come into place as you organize the steps to achieve your priorities.

3. Economize by working on what you can right now, and what you should target for later.

4. And lastly, you can contribute more when you realize your successes. The more you accomplish on YOUR priorities, the more you can build a foundation of success for others.

"Average people think merely of spending time. People focused on personal mastery ponder the wise use of it."

—*Mark Given*

How could I use the POSEC Method today to increase my levels of success? Who can I help by sharing my past successes?

_____

_____

_____

_____

_____

_____

_____

_____

_____

_____

_____

_____

_____

_____

_____

_____

_____

_____

_____

TRUST BASED
PHILOSOPHY

TRUST BASED
ACADEMY

TRUST BASED
COACHING

TIME MANAGEMENT AND THE POMODORO TECHNIQUE

The Pomodoro Technique was developed in the late 1980s by Francesco Cirillo while studying as a university student, and for many, the Pomodoro Technique has created higher levels of productivity.

In English, the word Pomodoro comes from the Italian word for ‹tomato’ and as simple as it may sound, Cirillo used a tomato-shaped kitchen timer as the basis for his system.

Using his system, you break your workday into 25-minute chunks separated by five-minute breaks…each chunk being called a **pomodoro**.

There are six steps in the original technique:

1. Decide on the task to be done.

2. Set the pomodoro timer (traditionally to 25 minutes).

3. Work undeterred and uninterrupted on the task.

4. End your work when the timer rings and put a checkmark on a piece of paper to show what you have completed.

5. If you have fewer than four checkmarks, take a short break (3–5 minutes), then go back to step #2.

6. If you complete four pomodoros while working on the same task, take a longer break (15–30 minutes), reset your checkmark count to zero, then go to step #1.

Cirillo suggests:

Each project should be handled with common sense... If you finish a task while the **Pomodoro** is still ticking, the following rules apply...

1. If a **Pomodoro** begins, continue until it rings.

2. It's a good idea to take advantage of the opportunity for overlearning, using the remaining portion of the **Pomodoro** to review or repeat what you've done, make small improvements, and note what you've learned until the Pomodoro rings and it is time for a break.

"Nothing is a waste of time if you use the experience wisely."

—Rodin

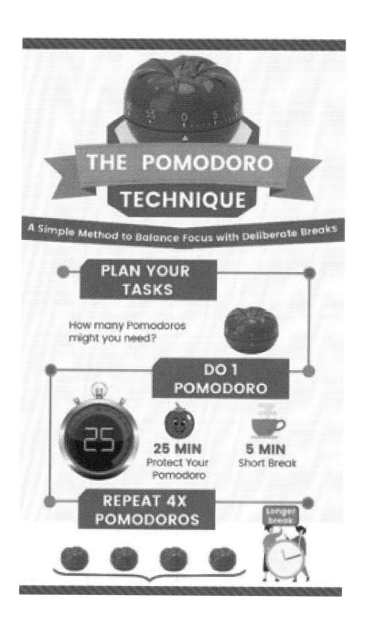

Have I ever tried a system similar to the Pomodoro Technique? Am I willing to try it out on an upcoming workday or project to see if it works for me? When will I do it and what project?

_____

_____

_____

_____

_____

_____

_____

_____

_____

_____

_____

_____

_____

_____

_____

_____

TIME MANAGEMENT AND THE EISENHOWER METHOD

The **Eisenhower Method**, also known as the **Eisenhower Matrix** or **Eisenhower Box**, is a method used to organize duties and tasks to help clarify priorities.

Similar to the Covey Principles, the **Eisenhower Method/ Eisenhower Matrix/Eisenhower Box** would best be described this way...

Each task in front of you is evaluated, then put into one of four quadrants described as:

important and urgent/important but not urgent /
not important but urgent/not urgent and not important.

Tasks that are important and urgent are completed immediately (do it now)

1. Tasks that are important but not urgent are assigned a completion date

2. Tasks that are not urgent are delegated

3. Tasks in the not important and not urgent quadrant are dropped or set aside entirely or until they become important (maybe never).

Dwight D. Eisenhower said it this way:

"What is important is seldom urgent and what is urgent is seldom important."

	URGENT	NOT URGENT
IMPORTANT	**DO IT NOW**	**PLAN IT**
NOT IMPORTANT	**DELEGATE**	**DROP IT**

Dwight D's time management and productivity system may not be the best and wisest system for you...but...it certainly worked for him.

You should at least consider that in a recent C-Span survey of historians, writers, and journalists rating Presidential effectiveness...Eisenhower was ranked as the 5th most effective President in the history of the US...not a bad rating considering there have been more than forty US Presidents. (Abraham Lincoln was considered the most effective with James Buchanan as the least).

"The common man is not concerned about the passage of time; the man of talent is driven by it."

—Shoppenhauer

How could I use the Eisenhower Method to immediately
be more effective?

_____

_____

_____

_____

_____

_____

_____

_____

_____

_____

_____

_____

_____

_____

_____

_____

TRUST BASED
PHILOSOPHY

TRUST BASED
ACADEMY

TRUST BASED
COACHING

THE STUDY OF PRE-CRASTINATION AND YOU

Possibly, you have heard one of these...

Measure twice, cut once...Marry in haste, repent at leisure... Look before you leap.

The opposite of procrastination can be a serious problem for many people also...possibly that's YOU?

It's a tendency called "pre-crastination".

Pre-crastination is the internal burning habit of completing tasks quickly just for the sake of getting things done sooner rather than later.

People struggling with pre-crastination answer emails immediately rather than carefully contemplating their replies. Others will pay bills as soon as they arrive, failing to collect additional interest income. And...there have been interesting studies that show pre-crastinators instinctively grabbing items when they first enter the grocery store, carrying them all the way to the back of the store, picking up more groceries at the back, then returning to the front of the store to pay and exit. Isn't it funny how these people will tote those items much farther than necessary...often lugging and dropping them along the way all that extra and unneeded distance?

If this sound like you, do not fear...here are:

5 ways to stop pre-crastinating

1. Lighten your load – remove everything from your to do list that is good, but not really necessary.

2. Schedule to do list – get realistic about the right time to check that item off your list and decide early when that right time is…then…commit to your schedule.

3. Schedule your to-be list too – regrets add stress to your life…so…get serious about scheduling items that will not stress you out at the end of your day, or the end of your week, or at the end of your life.

4. Schedule time to evaluate your progress. Utilizing the **Pomodoro Method** might be helpful here. Get each important task completed, then re-evaluate it so you do not get caught pre-crastinating.

5. Reflect at the end of the day. Some pre-crastination is productive. Think…how did I do and how can I improve. Reflection will help reduce stress and improve tomorrow's focus, possibly illuminating pre-crastination.

"The bad news is time flies. The good news is you are the pilot."

–Michael Altshuler

Am I a pre-crastinator? How can I use it as a benefit?

_____

_____

_____

_____

_____

_____

_____

_____

_____

_____

_____

_____

_____

_____

_____

_____

_____

_____

I have to have this RIGHT NOW!

MASTERING THE ART OF PRO-CRASTINATION

Maybe...you have heard one of these?

Do not put off until tomorrow what you can do today.

He who hesitates is last.

Procrastination is the thief of time.

Maybe...those were even written for YOU?

Joseph Ferrari, a professor of psychology at DePaul University is a pioneer of modern research on the subject of procrastination.

In his work, Joseph has found that as many as 20 percent of people are what he calls...chronic procrastinators.

But...I'm going to call on my good friend John Nimmo to explain the importance of this principle. John has written a wonderful book on pro-crastination that is worth your investment.

Here is what John would tell you...

There are three primary causes of procrastination.

1. Fear = we get frozen in our tracks because we are afraid something won't work. We might also be embarrassed that people will think we're a little crazy, or that someone will judge us, or that we might fall flat on our face.

2. Perfectionism = perfect is the enemy of adequate. It's true that we should always perform at our highest level, but perfect is sometimes not

possible no matter how much time and effort we invest. Be realistic about when enough is enough and perfection is not required. Sometimes, B or B+ work is just as valuable as A or A+ work.

3. Competing Interests = it is easy to procrastinate when you are not focused, so it is especially important to not have your hands in too many fires. When you do…you will often get burned!

"Every day, we must stand guard at the doorway of our mind. The subconscious seeks to derail our dreams by holding us hostage to sameness."

—John Nimmo

Are you stuck right now in procrastination because of fear, perfectionism, or competing interests? What will you do today to resolve your issue and no longer be a hostage?

_____

_____

_____

_____

_____

_____

_____

_____

_____

_____

_____

_____

_____

_____

_____

_____

_____

TRUST BASED
PHILOSOPHY

TRUST BASED
ACADEMY

TRUST BASED
COACHING

IS TIME NOT EARNING REALLY TIME WASTED?

earn

verb (used with object)

To gain or get in return for one's labor or service: to earn one's living.

To merit as compensation, as for service; deserve: to be worth more than one has earned.

To acquire through merit: to earn a reputation for honesty and trustworthiness.

To gain as due return or profit: Money, like behavior, earns interest.

To bring about or cause deservedly: I earned a special fishing trip with dad for washing his car.

It's often easy to think of earning as only money (and so much of the US defines it that way), but when you see it objectively, you recognize that earning is so much more than just money.

Take a good look at the definitions of earn again.

Only one is about a selfish desire to make more money. The others are about being worth more than you charged (high service creates high value), becoming the kind of person people want to associate with (that kind of earning will create long term relationships both personally and professionally), and being rewarded for the good you have provided others (the joy you receive from giving without focusing on a gain).

Reality…investing your time to earn (no matter how you define it) is never time wasted!

I love this poem and hope you learn from it as well…

This is the beginning of a new day.
God has given me this day to use as I will.
I can waste it or use it for good.
What I do today is important, because
I am exchanging a day of my life for it.
When tomorrow comes,
this day will be gone forever,
leaving in its place something
that I have traded for it.
I want it to be gain, not loss;
good not evil; success not failure;
in order that I shall not regret
the price I paid for it.

Author Unknown

**"A year from now you will wish
you had started today."**

—Karen Lamb

When I leave my home today, no matter what my personal circumstances, what 3 things will I do to better invest my time to receive the highest gain?

_____

_____

_____

_____

_____

_____

_____

_____

_____

_____

_____

_____

_____

_____

_____

_____

_____

_____

TRUST BASED
PHILOSOPHY

TRUST BASED
ACADEMY

TRUST BASED
COACHING

ARE YOU READING OR WATCHING?

While working on this book, I found some research you might find interesting.

Recent studies show that the average American actually has 5 hours and 14 minutes of free time every day.

And yet…4 out of 5 Americans still feel they do not have enough time to get things done.

We spend on average 3 ½ hours per day senselessly interacting with our phone.

And…interacting with your phone is much like gambling on a slot machine.

It can be both exhilarating and depressing!

So…the solution.

Why not read more every day (you've got the time).

If you would commit to cut out 1 hour each day of useless phone time, that would equal 365 hours per year.

If you divide that 365 hours by a 40-hour work week (treat it like work you love), you will see that you've added a full 9 weeks of productivity to your life each year.

How much might you learn?

How much could you grow?

How many new things would you have to share?

The truth…it's all YOUR choice.

Better than gambling on any slot machine and I would wager your winnings would be astronomical…I don't even need to study it!

"No matter what the season, one thing you can never recycle is time wasted."

—*Mark Given*

Begin by asking yourself...what trade magazine, blog, book, or electronic book will I read or listen to today in my extra 1 hour that could help me grow intellectually and/or financially?

_____

_____

_____

_____

_____

_____

_____

_____

_____

_____

_____

_____

_____

_____

_____

_____

TRUST BASED
PHILOSOPHY

TRUST BASED
ACADEMY

TRUST BASED
COACHING

APPLYING YOUR UNCERTAINTY CAPABILITY

It is often the...not knowing...that is the worst feeling of all.

Not knowing what to do, not knowing what's going to happen, not knowing what other people are thinking and feeling—these situations are ripe to breed anxiety in anyone...depending on how well an individual is able to tolerate **uncertainty.**

> **noun.**
>
> **Uncertainty** is defined as doubt. When you feel as if you are not sure (if you are not sure you can write that book...this is an **example of uncertainty)**. When the economy is soft or going sideways and causing everyone to worry about what will happen next (it's an **example** of **uncertainty**). When your GPS is telling you to go left, but you're just not convinced that it will be the shortest route and you think you know better (that's **uncertainty**).

Uncertainty...we all experience it. Sometimes we are frozen by it. And when it applies to time management and productivity, uncertainty can be debilitating.

Master-minds have said it this way...

"If I cease searching, then, woe is me, I am lost. That is how I look at it–keep going, keep going come what may." **—Vincent van Gogh**

"For all of its uncertainty, we cannot flee the future." **—Barbara Jordan**

"So what do we do? Anything. Something. So long as we just don't sit there. If we screw it up, start over. Try something else. If we wait until we've satisfied all the uncertainties, it may be too late." —**Lee Iacocca**

"The only thing that makes life possible is permanent, intolerable uncertainty; not knowing what comes next." —**Ursula K. Le Guin**

"If there's one thing that's certain in business, it's uncertainty." —**Stephen Covey**

So…whether you're certain or uncertain…take the time to plan that important first step. If it's unproductive, turn back and start again.

"When you are running down a path and you're certain that it's right, keep going because you can't help but stumble on some level of SUCCESS!"

—*Mark Given*

What am I involved in right now that makes me uncertain? When is the best 25 minutes today to schedule time to help me be clearer, plan my next step, and reduce my uncertainty?

_____

_____

_____

_____

_____

_____

_____

_____

_____

_____

_____

_____

_____

_____

_____

_____

TRUST BASED
PHILOSOPHY

TRUST BASED
ACADEMY

TRUST BASED
COACHING

THE 1ST RULE OF PRODUCTIVITY

The 1st Rule of Productivity: Get Things Done!

The 2nd Rule of Productivity: Just complete #1.

- A recent international study of the working population found that most workers face a distraction every eleven minutes, and once distracted, it takes 25 minutes to get back to the task at hand.

- A University of Michigan study showed that 20 to 40% of a worker's productivity is eaten up by task shifting (the time it takes to mentally reengage when shifting from one task to another)

- Research shows that distractions are a major cause of errors in healthcare, especially during the process of medication delivery. Yet, in the healthcare setting, distractions or interruptions are often expected as a "way we do business."

So…what IS productivity?

Well…according to Charles Duhigg, author of the New York Times Best Selling book The Power of Habit…it's getting the results you want with less time and effort. When you are trying to understand how to be productive, what you are really seeking is a way to achieve your goals while having time to spend on what matters.

The lesson here is...go back to Rule #1 so you will focus on being more productive and create the life you are seeking.

"The way to get started is to quit talking and begin doing."

—Walt Disney

What is one thing I could do differently every day beginning today so I can focus on Rule #1 to help create the life I really want?

_____

_____

_____

_____

_____

_____

_____

_____

_____

_____

_____

_____

_____

_____

_____

_____

_____

TRUST BASED
PHILOSOPHY

TRUST BASED
ACADEMY

TRUST BASED
COACHING

DEALING WITH YOUR OBSTACLE ILLUSIONS

Extraordinary success and productivity requires emotional competence, mental clarity and a willingness to disrupt your status quo. You must release low-level thinking that holds you back. To be a standout, you must cultivate your strengths and work through fear and doubt to manifest your ideas.

Emotional competence and mental clarity come from using two warriors...time and patience...to your advantage.

Let me better explain by sharing Psychologist Sherrie Campbell's *"Seven Step Process for dealing with your time management and productivity illusions"*.

1. Emotional management.

To be successful and productive...invest in internal growth and personal development. You have to be your own best manager. When mistakes happen, deal with the emotional consequences. Mistakes are the first steps in learning what has to change within you to achieve emotional balance and self-management. The better your self-knowledge, the more successful you will be.

Fear can prompt you to act too soon. Balance creates higher productivity and better allows you to manage your impulses.

Emotional management requires a more refined balance.

Successful entrepreneurs know when to be flexible and when to set limits. That emotional monitoring will make you an exceptional, high producing decision maker.

2. Have a purpose.

To be more productive and successful, you need a purpose you will follow through all the way to closure. A strong mission provides the <u>motivation</u> and belief to stand out. When you are clear about why you are investing your blood, sweat, tears, time, and energy there will be no room for laziness or complacency.

Time and patience keep you in touch with your commitment to succeed at all costs. Giving yourself time clears your mind and keeps you more grounded to your overall purpose. It prevents you from being an impulsive and low producing decision maker.

Time and patience supply you with a deep will to stay the course no matter how hard things get or no matter what challenges you face.

3. Rise above Conformity.

Exceptional entrepreneurs are nonconformists and are needed in a world that craves new ideas, thoughts, and inventions. They are unafraid to face the ridicule, the nay-sayers, and the rejections they will undoubtedly confront as they put their ideas to work.

Conformity can only get you where people and ideas have already been. You must think differently. Study entrepreneurs to learn what they did to help them succeed. Take seminars and learn to manage the worry and unconscious ways you sabotage your own <u>dream</u>. Trust that it could be YOUR idea that revolutionizes the world and produces a product that meets consumer needs.

Find the courage to take an idea that others may think crazy and make it possible. Take the impossible and make it possible.

4. Renew yourself.

It is easy to be passionate when you are starting out, but successful entrepreneurs commit to keeping their energy levels high when they hit the inevitable, frustrating roadblock. To be successful you have to care for yourself physically, emotionally, mentally and spiritually.

It is also important not to take things too seriously. That weakens your own emotional reserves. You have to bring a revitalized sense of renewed life into your business daily.

Your brain needs quality sleep, good nutrition and physical exercise to manage your thoughts and emotions. You have to keep your energy up. Taking time-out is crucial to staying fresh.

Stay healthy and focused. Keep in mind there is a one-to-one relationship between what you believe and what you receive. Never allow giving up to be an option.

5. Walk your talk.

You can talk about what you want to do so much that you develop an imaginary belief you have actually achieved your dream. To live your commitments, you must understand that "trying" is unproductive energy. It is a form of the fatalistic thinking pattern of "potential."

If you don't know how to do what you want to do, then take the time to learn more. At the end of the day you are responsible for making something happen. Remember, there is no such thing as being totally "ready." There will always be risk, so you must commit and put yourself in a position where success is your only choice.

There is one way to succeed: do what you say you are going to do. Talk is cheap...stalling takes a dream and shrinks it to a "thought." Excuses are dream-stealers that appear to have good intentions.

6. Remain curious.

Curiosity is a form of innocence and a protection from fear. Curiosity gives you the courage to start a business that will outperform status quo...it might even create a disruption. Find the courage to break boundaries…place your fear aside. Passionate curiosity is deeper than the fear of failure.

The "what if" state-of-mind has a natural energetic drive that helps you take risks you would normally not take. Oftentimes, the more we are told "no" the more curious we become to see what would happen if we did it anyway…the "what if".

Curiosity allows you to take your idea and go for it. Passionate curiosity can make the challenge of failure secondary. Success and disruption are possible, so why not risk it? The more curious you become, the more inspired you will be to test the limits of the impossible.

7. Doubt as motivation.

A little bit of doubt is healthy. Doubt means you are pushing yourself to the very edge of your comfort zone. Doubt can lead you to a place of discovery. Uncharted territory can create a mixture of excitement and doubt. Doubt can help you see the unforeseen and dig deeper into something you want to pursue.

Never believe any idea has reached its limit. Great entrepreneurs push past doubts, take what already exists and make it better. You have within you the ability to create something completely new.

To be a standout success, you must be radical enough to make your own rules…to be willing to rise above the status quo, and to have enough grit to take a risk.

"Glory lies in the attempt to reach one's goal and not in reaching it."
—Mahatma Ghandi

What is one obstacle that is holding me back from reaching my big success? How can I overcome it?

_____

_____

_____

_____

_____

_____

_____

_____

_____

_____

_____

_____

_____

_____

_____

_____

_____

_____

TRUST BASED
PHILOSOPHY

TRUST BASED
ACADEMY

TRUST BASED
COACHING

YOU GOTTA' DANCE UNTIL IT RAINS

Vic Johnson, author of the book *"Dance Until It Rains"*, begins his book with the story of a tribe in Africa that confounded many of the world's anthropologists.

It seems that this tribe had for centuries enjoyed a 100% success rate with its rain dance.

In comparing the tribe to the many other tribes that did rain dances (but who did not always experience success), the experts could not initially determine anything significant that differentiated the tribes.

They all performed the same rituals, they prayed the same incantations to the same gods, they wore much the same costumes.

Like all the tribes, they sometimes danced for days, often for weeks without pause.

But finally, an astute observer noticed something very telling.

The 100% successful tribe did one thing, and only one thing different that the other tribes did not do.

They ALWAYS kept dancing UNTIL it rained!

(HT to Tuesday Morning with Kathryn Scanland)

What does this mean for you? Well…what are you doing to make sure you have committed enough time AND enough energy to guarantee your success? Have you given up to soon and not seen the results you hoped for because you were not ALL IN?

Don't just dance <u>because you need it to rain</u>...commit the time, effort, and persistence to guarantee yourself that <u>you will not stop dancing UNTIL it rains</u>.

"Never mistake motion for action!"

–Ernest Hemingway

Write down one thing right now that you want so badly that you will not stop dancing UNTIL it rains!

_____

_____

_____

_____

_____

_____

_____

_____

_____

_____

_____

_____

_____

_____

_____

_____

_____

I understand you are tired,
but keep dancing UNTIL it rains!

PRODUCTIVITY REQUIRES INTENTION

pro·duc·tiv·i·ty

/ prō dək tivədē, prädək tivədē/   *noun*

the state or quality of producing something.

the effectiveness of productive effort as measured in terms of the rate of output per unit of input.   "Workers have boosted productivity by 30 percent"

in·ten·tion

/in ten(t)SH(ə)n/   *noun*

a thing intended; an aim or a plan.   "They were full of good intentions"

What have you been doing with your life?

Have productivity and intention been on your mind and you're trying desperately not to place yourself in a position of having regrets?

If that is you...it leads us to a belief (maybe it even proves) that productivity and intention are not just nouns...they are also verbs.

Almost every day, I begin my morning with reading, pondering, prayer, and then writing down a short list of goals for the best use of my time that day (my productivity, intentions and goals).

Results...

Often = highly intentional and productive (terrific things happen because of time well spent).

Occasionally = disappointing (I let myself get a little depressed or lethargic and frustration and laziness set in).

How about YOU?

Are YOU honest enough with yourself to decide what you want, write it down, get to work, then measure your progress?

We will never be out of the woods with these trying times so there is plenty of time to rebound.

If you are not where you want to be or where you should be TODAY (and very few are), why not join me?

Let's make the most of our opportunities.

YOU deserve the best the world has to offer and I believe I deserve it too...I'm in it to win it...how about YOU!!!

"Productivity and Results never appear by happenstance. It is the combination of focused intention, sincere effort, intelligent direction, and skillful execution."

–Mark Given

What is one thing I could be more intentional about TODAY to help me achieve my goal? What is one more productive way to help me get it?

_____

_____

_____

_____

_____

_____

_____

_____

_____

_____

_____

_____

_____

_____

_____

_____

TRUST BASED
PHILOSOPHY

TRUST BASED
ACADEMY

TRUST BASED
COACHING

WAITING AND WORRYING

It's easy for us to worry. The world is upside down, the slog continues, tragedies happen daily that are unevenly and widely distributed.

Worry takes a lot of effort.

Worry, unlike focus, learning and action, assists you accomplishing nothing of value.

And...at the same time, due to the time-horizon of the current world pandemic, it is also tempting to simply wait. Wait for things to get better...wait for things to get back to normal.

But all the time we spend waiting (for a normal that we may never see again) is time we're not spending learning, leading and connecting.

Waiting is actually a waste of time...and time flies by...so wasting time is actually a pretty shameful act.

If we decided to simply reduce our waiting and worrying allocation by 50%, just imagine how much we could discover, how many skills we could learn, how dramatically our attitude might shift.

We can still wait (time will pass either way). We can worry (even though it doesn't do any good). Perhaps though, we should concentrate more on how to wait and worry less?

"It is no good getting furious if you get stuck. What I do is keep thinking about the problem but work on something else."

—Stephen Hawking

What is one thing I am worried about right now that I have no control over? Where could I better place my negative energy with positive energy?

_____

_____

_____

_____

_____

_____

_____

_____

_____

_____

_____

_____

_____

_____

_____

_____

_____

TACTIC VS STRATEGY

A tactic is a method or technique used to achieve an immediate or short-term gain

- A strategy is a carefully defined and detailed plan to achieve a long-term goal
- Every year...the Golden State Warriors have a winning strategy as do the Cleveland Cavaliers.

In 2016, the Chicago Cubs proved they had a winning strategy... it was called World Series Champions!

Many Olympians fine tune their winning strategy every time they prepare for the Olympic Games.

Disney has a well-oiled and diversified winning business strategy...and it seems to be working well for them.

You may not like Wal-Mart, but they have a clearly defined and powerful winning strategy that made them the #1 retailer in the world until Amazon came along with a better strategy.

A couple of years ago, I decided I wanted to get the book I wrote with Don Greeson, *"Finding My Why Ernie's Journey...A Tale for Seekers"* into more hands and sought out assistance to maximize downloads on Amazon as a strategy.

With unanticipated results, our book was not only downloaded a lot the first week of the new strategy, but on Thursday, May 19, 2016 it hit #1 in the Amazon Kindle Store...in two different categories (motivational and self-help).

That may not make Don Greeson and me famous New York Times Best Selling Authors, but it ain't to shabby too be an ***Amazon #1 Best Selling Author!***

The tactic was to share Ernie's story of hope and positive energy with more people.

Our winning strategy though…thanks to hundreds of people just like you, pushed it to #1 (even if only for two days).

If you were one of those downloads in 2016…thank-you with words and emotions of sincere gratitude!

"Strategy without tactics is the slowest route to victory. Tactics without strategy is the noise before defeat."

—Sun Tzu

When I get up each morning, am I focused on tactics (short term gains) or strategy (long term goals)? I will take a good look at my hourly schedule today and determine...is there something I could be doing better beginning immediately that would help me better achieve my long-term goals?

_____

_____

_____

_____

_____

_____

_____

_____

_____

_____

_____

_____

_____

_____

_____

_____

_____

_____

TRUST BASED
PHILOSOPHY

TRUST BASED
ACADEMY

TRUST BASED
COACHING

PRODUCTIVITY AND VIDEO INTERFACING

The world has changed so dramatically that it is really a little ridiculous to think we can live and work without immersing ourselves in a world of virtual contact.

But...whenever you can...choose physical over digital.

You don't even have to take my word for it...Satya Nadella, the CEO of Microsoft, said it this way...

"We are moving from a world where computing power was scarce to a place where it now is almost limitless, and where the true scarce commodity is increasingly human attention!"

The wise businessperson will schedule time every single day to connect with his clients because no matter what product you manufacture or whatever service you provide, you still need people to buy it.

The spouse or friend or child that wants to be loved will invest the time needed to produce a deep and positive emotional connection which will guarantee years of happiness for all the people involved.

It is still a fact of life and business...video is great, virtual is cool... but technology has still not replaced the human connection (and I'm pretty confident that it won't during my lifetime).

"Tomorrow becomes never. No matter how small the task, take the first step now!"

—Tim Ferris

Who is one person I need to connect with today? Do I have a written list of my most important clients right in front of me, so I see it everyday and connect with each one of them often?

THE WORLD MIGHT DEFINE YOU BY YOUR ERRORS, BUT DON'T LET THAT STOP YOU FROM ACHIEVING

During the 1985 baseball season, Bill Buckner emerged as the Red Sox stalwart first baseman, starting all 162 games and shattering his own big league record with 184 assists.

Toward the end of the 1986 season, Bill was afflicted with leg injuries and struggled throughout the playoffs, but his tenth-inning error in Game 6 of the 1986 World Series against the New York Mets remains one of the most memorable plays in baseball history.

That error was long considered part of a curse on the Red Sox that kept them from winning the World Series, and led to years of fan anger and public mockery, but Bill Buckner handled the criticism graciously and was finally embraced by Red Sox fans again after their 2004 World Series victory.

After spending his last few seasons with the California Angels, Kansas City Royals, and a second stint with the Red Sox, Buckner became the 21st player in MLB history to play in four decades, ending his career with 2,715 hits and 498 doubles, having batted over .300 seven times with three seasons of 100 runs batted in (RBI).

He never struck out 40 times in a season and he finished with the fifth-lowest strikeout rate among players whose careers began after 1950. Bill Buckner led his league in assists four times, with his 1985 mark remaining the American League (AL) record.

Bill retired with the fourth-most assists by a first baseman (1,351) in major league history, despite not playing the position regularly until he was 27 years old.

But…Bill never gave up and he never gave in…he was dedicated to winning. After Buckner retired from baseball, he moved his family to Idaho where he invested in real estate in the Boise area. One of the housing subdivisions that he developed is still named "Fenway Park".

And here is the best part…

On April 8, 2008, Bill Buckner threw out the first pitch to former teammate Dwight Evans at the Red Sox home opener as they unfurled their 2007 World Series championship banner. He received a two-minute standing ovation from the sell-out crowd.

It may not ever be a movie, but to me, this story is golden.

And you should never let the world define you either. Do what you have got to do to fight through the fear and you never know…you may just get that standing ovation too!

"You cannot kill time without injuring eternity."
—*Henry David Thoreau*

What is one thing that is holding me back from the standing ovation I know I deserve?

_____

_____

_____

_____

_____

_____

_____

_____

_____

_____

_____

_____

_____

_____

TRUST BASED
PHILOSOPHY

TRUST BASED
ACADEMY

TRUST BASED
COACHING

ARE YOU FARMING?

Farmers plant and they expect a harvest.

They know that they know that they know...that when they plant...they get results.

Do you have that kind of unshakable confidence, that unmovable expectation of productivity, those time management skills to maximize the seasons?

When you schedule time to plant seeds...those seeds don't just grow...they produce more seeds.

So...be like the farmer.

Plant, nurture, watch those seeds grow...then enjoy an abundance of new seeds.

Right now is a GREAT time to plant more seeds.

When we do...we can EXPECT a fruitful harvest.

I'm ready for that...how 'bout YOU!

"Tomorrow is the most important thing in life. Comes into us at midnight very clean. It's perfect when it arrives, and it puts itself in our hands. It hopes we have learned something from yesterday."

—John Wayne

What seeds should I be planting TODAY to guarantee the harvest I am seeking?

_____

_____

_____

_____

_____

_____

_____

_____

_____

_____

_____

_____

_____

_____

_____

_____

TRUST BASED
PHILOSOPHY

TRUST BASED
ACADEMY

TRUST BASED
COACHING

YOUR MEASURING SYSTEM

I tried to recharge the lithium battery that works with my drill. After twenty minutes, the charger said the battery had failed.

Fortunately, I have a second battery. I put that into the charger and it also showed a failure.

Actually…neither battery had failed. The charger had.

(HT Seth Godin)

The only way you will know if your time management systems are working are if you measure them.

The only way you will improve your productivity is to observe more clearly what you are doing and how you are currently doing it.

Some years ago, I wrote in a little pad that I always keep in my right pocket…*"Things that get measured, get improved…or removed"*, and that statement is just as applicable today as it was when I wrote it.

It is only when we engage in measuring that solutions to our problems appear.

A masterpiece can be created by what YOU do with your time and what time does with YOU…

"Masterpieces are not measured in daily activities alone, but through a lifetime of gentle brush strokes!"

So…what are you painting today, this week, this month, this year, and throughout your life?

You will only see the results you are seeking when you take the time to measure.

**"Success doesn't just happen…
it comes as a calculated result
of a strategic focus."**

—*Mark Given*

After measuring my schedule from yesterday, what is one thing I could have done differently to improve my brush strokes and have painted a different (possibly much better) picture?

_____

_____

_____

_____

_____

_____

_____

_____

_____

_____

_____

_____

_____

_____

_____

_____

TRUST BASED
PHILOSOPHY

TRUST BASED
A C A D E M Y

TRUST BASED
C O A C H I N G

YOU ARE NOT DOING IT ALONE

Whether you are a leader, a manager, a salesperson, or a servant, it nearly always takes more than just you alone to perform at your highest level.

You are reading this book...so it is, of course, expected that you would perform at a high level.

Why not surround yourself with people that help you prepare and perform.

If you are honest with yourself, you know that you are not doing it alone, and you can't compete doing it alone.

I bet you've done it though.

You thought it would be easier to do something without getting help...

You tried to screw in that screw with only your fingernail...

You tried lifting something you should not have because you didn't want to burden someone...

Who knows...maybe you even tried paddling your canoe with only your hands...

If you're like me, you struggle asking.

And yet...nothing worthwhile was ever accomplished alone.

Ask for HELP...get some help!

You are surrounded by good people that want to help and tools that were created to help.

All you have to do is ask.

When you do…you'll be blessed for asking and those people… the people that willingly serve you…well, they will be even more blessed than you.

Give them an opportunity to HELP…you will both be grateful and rewarded.

So…here are a couple of good questions…

Do you have a practice group that meets weekly or monthly?

Do you have mentors that help you perform at your highest level?

Do you have a coach that keeps you focused and progressing?

Success…you are NOT doing it alone!

**"You must remain focused on
your journey to greatness."**

—*Les Brown*

Is there a goal or a project I am working on (right now) that could turn out better if I asked for help? Who will I ask?

_____

_____

_____

_____

_____

_____

_____

_____

_____

_____

_____

_____

_____

_____

_____

_____

TRUST BASED
PHILOSOPHY

TRUST BASED
ACADEMY

TRUST BASED
COACHING

THE SECRET QUESTION YOU SHOULD BE ASKING YOURSELF ABOUT PRODUCTIVITY

What is the secret to insane productivity?

You might be asking yourself this question since you invested in yourself and chose to read this book.

So...here's the answer to your secret question.

Obsessing about productivity is not going to make you work smarter or longer.

In fact, there is plenty of research to show that working more does not always guarantee success...and very often doesn't.

Sometimes (and more often than not) ...working less will actually produce better results.

You might ask yourself...what could I do to break the overworking cycle...well...take the advice of these masters and you might just have your answer!

- Leonardo da Vinci took multiple naps a day and slept less at night.

- The French emperor Napoleon was not shy about taking naps. He indulged daily.

- Although Thomas Edison was embarrassed about his napping habit...he practiced this ritual on a daily basis.

- Eleanor Roosevelt, the wife of President Franklin D. Roosevelt, chose to boost her energy before speaking engagements…by napping.

- Gene Autry, "The Singing Cowboy," routinely took naps in his dressing room between performances.

- President John F. Kennedy ate his lunch in bed and then settled in for a nap—every day!

- Oil industrialist and philanthropist John D. Rockefeller napped every afternoon in his office.

- Winston Churchill's afternoon nap was non-negotiable. He believed it helped him get twice as much done each day.

- President Lyndon B. Johnson took a nap every afternoon at 3:30 p.m. so he could break his day up into "two shifts."

- Though he was criticized for it, President Ronald Reagan famously took naps as well. (HT CamMi Pham)

So…herein lies the answer to your secret question.

Do YOU want to be highly productive…?

Why not…take a nap!

"Working on the right thing is more important than working hard."

—*Caterina Fake*

It might be hard to imagine, and I may not believe it will work, but what would be the BEST TIME for me to take a daily 20 minute nap to refresh my brain and improve my focus? How do I need to change my schedule to get that done?

_____

_____

_____

_____

_____

_____

_____

_____

_____

_____

_____

_____

_____

_____

TRUST BASED
PHILOSOPHY

TRUST BASED
ACADEMY

TRUST BASED
COACHING

6 SECRETS TO MASTERING PRODUCTIVITY

So...maybe there is no way I can convince you that you should take a nap and you are looking for a different conclusion to mastering your Time Management and Productivity problem?

If that's you...here are six other secrets to mastering productivity:

1. Touch it once = if you touch it, take action immediately – email can be the death of good time management.

2. Make more lists = stick to the six most important things you need to get done that day and avoid letting all the small fires stop you in your tracks.

3. Plan how much time you will allocate to each task = if the task is too big to accomplish that day, write down how much time each day to dedicate to it until you get it done.

4. Plan the day = then stick to that schedule no matter what. Someone else's priority does not always have to become your priority.

5. Prioritize = If you have five things on your list, decide which one is the top priority (and so on) and don't let the other four prevent you from accomplishing number one.

6. Ask yourself "Will it hurt me to throw this away" = 80% of all filed or stored information is never referred to again, so purge those files immediately.

"Your time becomes unbelievably profitable when you use it fully with your most productive intentions!"

—Mark Given

Of these six productive habits, at which one can I be better?
Which one will I better implement immediately?

_____

_____

_____

_____

_____

_____

_____

_____

_____

_____

_____

_____

_____

_____

_____

_____

_____

_____

ONE LAST MESSAGE FROM MARK

Thank-you!

My good friend, Zan Monroe, once said, "What you focus on expands" and I have witnessed that to be true over and over in the life of others and in my own life.

In brief definition, Zan meant that the things you concentrate your time and talents on become the things that are most important to you, and they become what you are known for.

Trust is one of those things I want to be known and respected for and I believe it either is or should be for you too.

Why?

Because, when the people you love the most really and deeply trust you, your life is filled with joy. When your friends trust you, your life becomes fun. When the people you lead trust you, things get accomplished and when your clients and customers trust you, you create financial security and wealth.

So, thank-you for taking your valuable time to invest in you by reading this book...but reading is just the first step.

Now, you should go out and actually apply it every day.

You can do it...and the time to start is now!

I am just one of the people rooting for your SUCCESS, so go get a piece of paper right now and write down where and how you're going to begin improving your Time Management and Productivity skills and building more Trust.

Then…when it's convenient, drop me a note or an email and let me know how it all worked out for you. Please share with me **YOUR SUCCESS STORY.** I always love hearing success stories, and with your permission, it might just make my next book!

BOOK
BONUS

TRUST BASED PHILOSOPHY BOOK BONUS

10 More Southern Hospitality Secrets

1. **RSVP in a timely manner** = That friend of yours already knows you are busy, but come on…how in the world is your friend supposed to plan enough food and enough beverages if you won't be kind enough to RSVP. Sometimes you need to make a commitment and stick with it. Come to the party, or don't, but be kind enough to let them know in a timely manner. Don't YOU deserve and expect the same treatment?

2. **Taking off your sunglasses indoors** = I suppose it's ok if you run into a store or convenience store to grab something…but…when you are communicating with others, take off your sunglasses so they can see your eyes. If you're as cool as Jack Nicholson, you get a free pass on this one, but really… who else is as cool as Jack? Take them off!

3. **Show some gratitude for those little acts of service** = How much time does it really take to say "thankyou"… about a second! Get your face out of your phone, stop talking to that business associate of yours and acknowledge that someone is alive and right in front of you! And if the kindness was really kind…a small gift might be appropriate. It's all about how you make other people feel that elevates your life and your business.

4. **Dealing patiently with that long line** = You hate it and I do too, but nonetheless…part of life is standing in line and waiting in traffic. Take a deep breath and stop crowding. Hold on a minute before you cut someone off and infuriate them. Remember that they are having to wait too! Is your

life really so overwhelmed that you have to ignore the rest of the human race just so YOU can save an extra minute? Slow down…be a little kinder…maybe even smile or speak to the other people waiting. When you do, you WILL feel better and you get a lot closer to building trust.

5. **Holding the elevator door (do not push that button!)** = You might have done this. You walked into the elevator, pushed your floor button, then immediately pushed the close door button…really? If you think about it, that's a bit selfish and a little bit arrogant. How about not forgetting the time you were lugging your luggage down the corridor and some lone passenger closed the door on you…leaving YOU to wait 5 minutes for the next elevator. YOU can do better…YOU can be better! Next time…press your floor button and let the elevator door close on its own. It may not make you feel better, but to the person that just slipped into your elevator, you'll come across much kinder!

6. **Being on time** = Most people I know struggle with this (and I do too from time to time) …but being on time for your appointment shows respect and builds trust. There is something very frustrating about showing up on time, then having to wait for the late comers…especially when you already know who has a regular habit of being late and they are late again. Don't YOU be that person! Today is just as good a day as any to overcome your problem. Make a commitment with yourself right now to correct the problem and start being on time…regularly!

7. **Opening doors for women (and men)** = Even during my life, I've experienced a distant time when opening the door for someone else was the rule, not the exception. But…the world has changed. That does not mean YOU have to ignore this simple kindness. I've frantically grabbed at doors before they closed in my face so many times over the last decade that it makes me sad. Sad for the loss of hospitality, sad for the desire to do a good deed, and sad

for the lack of such little effort that should be common…
even if it's not just Southern. Even the excuse that women
want equality doesn't flush with me. Opening the door
is just common courtesy and if some person appears
offended by the kindness, that's their problem…not
yours. So…here's a simple question…would you open the
door for your mamma? Of course you would…so why not
just get in the habit of doing it for others too…always!

8. **Remembering the important little words** = Thankyou,
   you're welcome, please, grateful, appreciate, blessing,
   happy, smile, beautiful, giving, accept, generous,
   handsome, how are you, I am indebted to you, you are an
   inspiration to me, …the list could go on, and there are some
   little words that will mean more to YOU than others…so…
   all you have to remember is that kind words are like honey!

9. **Asking permission first** = Of course it is true that on
   occasion, it's better to push forward and ask forgiveness
   later…but more often, it is to your benefit and for your
   benefit to ask permission. We've all experienced the
   disappointment of someone screwing it up when they
   (and YOU) could have avoided all the pain if they had
   just asked. It's a southern thing for sure…ask your mama
   or your papa before you shoot at something that you
   should not be shootin' at…they know better than you!

10. **Minding your own business** = For some people, it
    is nearly impossible to do. But not YOU…or please…
    if it is…get your opinion, or your suggestion, or your
    experience, and your mouth out of my business unless
    I ask you for help. That method has not worked since
    caveman days, so why in the world would you think
    sticking your nose in my business would work today…
    if I need your help and when it becomes painful
    enough to do something different…I'll ask you. Sticking
    your nose in my business is how wars begin!

TRUST BASED
PHILOSOPHY

TRUST BASED
ACADEMY

TRUST BASED
COACHING

ADDITIONAL BOOK BONUS

MARK GIVEN INTERVIEWED BY JACK CANFIELD

Jack Canfield, Co-Creator, #1 NY Times Best-Selling Book Series Chicken Soup for the Soul®

Jack Canfield: Hi. I'm Jack Canfield, co-author of the New York Times number one best-selling series, *Chicken Soup for the Soul*, co-author of *The Success Principles*, and a featured teacher in the movie, *The Secret*. I'm sitting here today in an interview with Mark Given. I find Mark to be one of the more interesting and fun people I've ever interacted with, so I'm looking forward to our interview today.

Mark Given: Thank you.

Jack Canfield: Let's start with this, just tell our viewers a little bit about who you are and what you do.

Mark Given: Well, Jack, I've spent nearly 40 years studying the science and the art of building trust. I've written several books on this important subject, directed towards trust based leadership, trust based selling, and trust based success. I travel the country doing mostly keynotes and breakout sessions, half day, or full day sessions, sometimes multi-day sessions on teaching the four steps, or the four stages of trust to companies, and organizations, and associations, and groups that want to succeed by understanding the importance of building trust with their customers and clients, or with their staff, with their employees, with all the people they serve, even their own families.

It's fun. It's exciting. It's interesting to see people when the lights come on and they realize that trust is the foundation of everything. When people lose trust, it's difficult to rebound.

It is so very important that we teach these four stages of trust that are critical to success and are relevant to what all of us do.

Jack Canfield: I'm going to ask you about those four stages in a moment.

Mark Given: Good.

Jack Canfield: But, before I do that. I know you're very passionate about what you do. How did you get into trust being your focus? Why are you so passionate about it?

Mark Given: Well, Jack, there are probably a lot of reasons for that. First of all, when I graduated from college, all I really wanted to do was be in business. So, I went into retail for 20 years and had a pretty successful company in North Carolina, and Virginia. What I discovered was that if my employees didn't trust me, they would steal from me. If customers didn't like us and trust us, they would just do business with somebody else. I eventually sold that company and got into real estate. I discovered it was exactly the same thing with my customers, and clients, and all of the other people I worked with within the real estate industry.

When there's no trust, it's very difficult to succeed.

On top of all that and probably the most important thing personally is that my lovely bride of 40 years and I have five children, and we meant to do that.

I've discovered in life that maintaining trust with your spouse and with your children is critical to happiness and success. It's tough to be successful in any portion of your life when there's no foundation of trust.

I started studying that years ago, not realizing that I was studying the art and the science of trust, but I began by reading books. Books like yours Jack, *Chicken Soup for the Soul*. Many of the stories you included talk about trust, and love, and care and how people feel.

The Success Principles has many of the same principles. There are many other good, really powerful books, that in theory cover the art of building trust.

But I've also discovered that there are no tricks to it. It's just a simple, yet not simplistic science and an art to understanding how to be trustworthy. How you can show people that they can really count on you and care about you and that you care about them.

It's been exciting to spend all these years really studying the art and science of trust and developing some clarity on the 4 Stages of Trust.

Jack Canfield: You know it's funny. I hadn't thought of this in years, but I'm a human potential trainer.

Mark Given: Yes, of course you are.

Jack Canfield: I do workshops and so on. One of the first workshops I ever took was with a guy named Jack Gibb who wrote a book called Trust. He taught this model called TORI. Trust, T-O-R-I, trust leads to openness, openness leads to self-realization and realization of others, and that leads to interdependence and independence instead of co-dependence and dominate dependence.

Mark Given: Sure. That's correct.

Jack Canfield: That's so cool. Thank you for reminding me of one of the major pillars of my own consciousness.

Mark Given: That's terrific. I'm glad I could help just a little.

Jack Canfield: We talked about the 4 Stages of Trust. Talk about that a little bit.

Mark Given: Well, what we've discovered in our own studies is there is nothing else out there similar to what we've done, to individualize these 4 Stages of Trust.

But, there really are 4 stages.

The first stage is *The Introduction Stage*, or what I call, the *Grand Opening*.

There are several studies by highly respected Universities now that show people make a decision about you and me in 38 to 55 milliseconds. We've formed the same opinions just as other people form an opinion of us. We decide and they decide whether they like us or can trust us in less than a blink of the eye.

They decide whether they want to associate with us, or do business with us. They decide whether they want to be around us or not be around us that quickly.

And, the Grand Opening is just the 1st critical stage of trust.

The million dollar question then is; *how do we perform at a high enough level so we always have our best Grand Opening ready to deliver to everyone we meet…anytime…anywhere?*

The 2nd Stage of Trust is also very important. We call that the *Rapport Building Stage*.

Stage 2 is where we get to know people. It's really more about learning to ask good questions and then really listening for the answers. There's an old Chinese proverb that says, "Listen with the intent to hear."

What I've discovered is that when we spend more time asking and then really listening, we become a friend and a confidant.

It is amazing how much we can learn about people and how you build a foundation of trust by just listening and not talking.

Jack Canfield: My wife always says to me, "You want to focus on being more inter-rested than being interesting."

Mark Given: That's right.

Jack Canfield: Exactly.

Mark Given: You go a lot further by being interested.

Jack Canfield: Exactly.

Mark Given: Then, the 3rd Stage of Trust is the *Maintenance Stage*.

That's where we do all the things that are important to maintain trust. We do that by serving and being more of a giver than a taker.

We all know people that are givers. They are the kind of people we want to associate with. The 3rd stage is all the skills necessary to become more giving.

Bob Burg and John David Mann wrote a wonderful book that reflects this stage perfectly.

It's called *The Go-Giver*. A very simple, yet powerful book.

Jack Canfield: I know, I've read that.

Mark Given: But this principle is also really profound. I've gotten to know both Bob and John for that reason. It's such an important book. It's being a giver instead of a taker. The world is full of takers.

Then, the 4th Stage of Trust is the one that we all need because sometimes we mess up, no matter how good we are, how smart we are.

It's the *Apology Stage* or what I also call the *Repair Stage*.

This stage is the science and the study of how to apologize. How do you repair the damage once you've made a mistake?

That really relates to companies as well as people. I mean, gosh, how many articles are there every day now, online about some company or individual that has damaged trust with their customers or associates, or the country or the world. It relates to business. It relates to life and it relates to our own personal relationships with the people we care about.

Those are the four important stages, and they're very separate because the skills necessary for each are very different. That's why I spend the time teaching people and speaking to people about how to be their best in each of the four stages.

Jack Canfield: Now I wish I had three hours, I'd literally attack all four of those in-depth. But, I will ask you one follow-up question. You talked about the 1st Stage and the **Grand Opening**, and you only have 55 milliseconds. That's 55 thousandths of a second.

Mark Given: That's right.

Jack Canfield: Which is like, how do you even measure that? But, give us a clue about how you, in that 55 thousandths of a second, what can, or should, someone do?

Mark Given: Well, of course it begins with the way you look. It's your facial expressions. It's the way you dress. Those are the simple things, the obvious things.

But I've discovered a more complex process. It's what we do in our verbal opening.

We've all been taught a standard opening or greeting. We call that a two-step greeting. It's goes......Hi, I'm ......

That introduction is focused on ourselves. It's all about ME.

What I've learned in all these years of research is that when we teach people to go from a two-step greeting to a three-step greeting that it changes the way people feel about us. And the bonus is that we actually listen better. It actually subliminally demonstrates interest in the other person.

As simple as that may sound, it's not simplistic. When we're teaching the **Grand Opening**, we spend some time teaching people to go from a two-step greeting to a three-step greeting, which opens up a whole new realm of trust. And the magic is that we do it in just the very first few seconds of meeting someone new.

It can also be used with people we already know well. As is said in some circles, the 3 Step Opening is a game changer.

Jack Canfield: What are those three-steps?

Mark Given: The three-steps are simple. You go from, it's all about me to it's really about you. And I mean that literally.

In other words, instead of saying, "Hi, I'm me." You would say, "Hi, it's good to see YOU (or something similar). I appreciate the opportunity for us to be here, Jack. Thank YOU for doing this. Then, I'd share my name."

We would actually use the word, YOU twice, instead of making it quickly about yourself.

Jack Canfield: Yeah, I hear that.

Mark Given: Instead of hey, or hi, or hello, I'm me. It's hello. It's good to see YOU. Thank YOU for interviewing me. Boy, sure appreciate YOUR time today.

When I get done with the three-steps, or the initial two-steps, then I get to the "I'm Mark Given."

But, what we've also found as a bonus is that when people go from a two-step greeting to a three-step greeting, they more often walk away and actually remember the name of the person that they just were introduced to.

Jack Canfield: Interesting.

Mark Given: Often, when you use the two-step greeting, you walk away and you forget. Now, what was her name again? We take memory courses and try to do all these things, and just going from a two-step greeting to a three-step greeting is a remarkable change in the science of trust, building trust and creating an immediate likeable bound.

Jack Canfield: That's fascinating. I'd love to interview you about all this. I'll have to take your course! And I can tell that you are passionate about this.

Mark Given: I am.

Jack Canfield: You've talked about why you're so passionate about it. There are a lot of people talking about trust. I know Stephen M.R. Covey and others. What makes your work different?

Mark Given: Well, what we've learned is there's really not a single person, there's not a company, or an association, or organization out there that has not benefited from our programs and teaching steps. Instead of just a concept of building trust, we actually teach people how to do it.

Jack Canfield: How to do it and it is needed.

Mark Given: And we teach the steps on how to do it. We do it in those different formats, in a keynote, or breakout, or a half for full-day session, so that we can actually delve into those 4 different Stages of Trust and teach them the techniques. There are a lot of motivational speakers out there, and certainly, we motivate, but the difference, I feel, and what makes me so passionate about this is, when I'm out speaking and I see the lights come on in their brain and they think, "Oh, I could use that. How did I not know that, or how did I miss that, or gosh, I just made that mistake, or I said something or I did something and here's how I fix it."

It's really exciting to get those emails, or a note, or something from somebody that says, "Thanks for teaching me that. Thanks for helping. Here's what happened as a result. I went home and did this, or I had a customer or client, my best client, that I really messed it up and I've been able to repair that because of these important techniques."

It's exciting to get up in the morning and get out and do what I do, because this changes lives. It changes businesses.

Jack Canfield: You know, it's so sad that our schools don't teach these skills.

Mark Given: Sure. I agree.

Jack Canfield: I always tell people, "Tell me the five causes of the civil war." No one can even remember them, but we study that for days, or weeks.

But, we're not learning communication skills, relationship skills, self-management skills.

It's like we have to go into the hotels and the conference centers to learn what's really important. You're out there doing that. That's great. When you look at the clients you have, are there common challenges that people are facing out there in relation to this? How do you help them address those?

Mark Given: Yes, Jack. What I've found is that we all make mistakes. We all want the same thing and that's to build trust with people. People that we care about, or people we want to associate with, or people we want to do business with.

The real challenge is that we all experience much of the same thing. We have good days and we have bad days. When we have those bad days, we need some methods to improve and to repair. Just look at the statistics on marriages these days and you can see that clearly, there's a need for what I do and have studied. Although, I spend the majority of my time in the business world, the relationship world, marital world, could also use the techniques and skills too.

It's really exciting and fun to get out and help people see that they can do it. It's not about what I've learned, or sharing some things, it's what they can actually go and apply immediately themselves.

Jack Canfield: I'm sure you find too, like from my work, if I do a corporate training, the people take those same skills home with their wife, with their neighbors, in their church, with their children.

Mark Given: Sure, absolutely.

Jack Canfield: Absolutely, very good. If someone's sitting out there watching this, they're probably thinking, "Yeah, I don't know all that stuff about phases of trust and how to do it and I've lost some business because of, perhaps, betraying a trust, or not knowing how to build that rapport and trust." They're thinking about, perhaps, hiring you to work with them. What would you tell them?

Mark Given: I'd say, "Please, give me a call."

Jack Canfield: Plain and simple.

Mark Given: Please give me a call, because I'm pretty confident that there's something, whether you're a leader and trying to build trust with your organization, your staff, or your employees, or whether you're a sales person trying to build trust with your clients or customers, or you're just trying to build a successful life.

What I would say is that we have some things that can help you. That, given even just a little bit of time, we can share important trust building systems that people can apply immediately. So they can go home or back to work and actually do something.

What's fun is to see people actually go home and do something. So, call me, they can reach me at MarkGiven.com. It's really easy to find me and I invite anyone that could benefit to do that.

Jack Canfield: You're not in the witness protection program.

Mark Given: I'm not, thank goodness, you can find me.

Jack Canfield: Very good, very good. Well, Mark, this is fascinating. I think trust is critical ... It's a foundational thing, that everything else is built on. If you don't have it, nothing moves forward. Thanks for being my guest today. I really appreciate it.

Mark Given: My pleasure Jack, absolutely my pleasure.

Jack Canfield: If you want to build more trust in your relationships, in your organization, if you want to teach your people, whether they're sales people, managers, whatever it might be, at your association meeting, or convention, your conference, an in-house workshop, whatever, Mark Given can help you do that. Check out his website at MarkGiven.com.

TRUST BASED
PHILOSOPHY

TRUST BASED
ACADEMY

TRUST BASED
COACHING

MOTIVATE AND INSPIRE OTHERS!

"Share This Book"

Retail $24.95

Special Quantity Discounts

5-20 Books	$21.95
21-99 Books	$18.95
100-499 Books	$15.95
500-999 Books	$10.95
1,000+ Books	$8.95

To Place an Order Contact:
(252) 536-1169
www.MarkGiven.com

"If you are looking for a speaker, trainer and coach that can empower, inspire, and motivate your group, then you must book my friend Mark Given!"

THE IDEAL PROFESSIONAL SPEAKER FOR YOUR NEXT EVENT!

Any organization that wants to develop their people to become "extraordinary," needs to hire Mark for a keynote and/or workshop training!

—James Malinchak, Featured on ABC's "Secret Millionaire"
Best Selling Author of 20 Books

"We hire Mark to share his Trust Based Philosophy in leadership, sales and **success with our 1500 members every year!"**
—Zan Monroe, CEO Long Leaf Pine Association,
Author, Speaker and Coach

"You are simply an event planners dream! I have been involved with

contracting hundreds of speakers for various programs over the last 24+ years and I consider you an exemplary example of an ideal speaker."
—Rebecca Fletcher, Director, GIRE, VP of Education

Book Mark to Speak, Teach, Consult, or Coach:

(252) 536-1169

mark@markgiven.com

www.MarkGiven.com

In addition to my immediate family, I am grateful to all these people (and more). They have inspired me to strive to become the best Mark Given I can become:

Bob Burg	Jeffrey Gitomer	Jon Gordon
John David Mann	Ric Moore	Tom Peters
James Malinchak	John Nimmo	Richard Paul Evans
Jack Canfield	Gary Zhou	Robin Sharma
Darren Hardy	Seth Godin	Daniel Pink
Kevin Harrington	Frankie Jones	Murphy Myrick, Jr
Les Brown	Paula Jones	George Conner
Zan Monroe	Bud Nelson	Mark Evans
Og Mandino	Karen Nelson	Cindy Evans
Napoleon Hill	Patti Aubrey	Bert Fortier
Don Greeson	Lori Garrett	Melinda Fortier
Joe Theismann	Jeff Garrett	Lili Paulk
Cindy McLane	Austin Moore	Hyrum Smith
Jeffrey R Holland	Chuck Gallagher	Joseph Smith
Russel M Nelson	Janice Porter	Daniel Pink
Dave Evans	Jerry Rossi	Julie Carrier
Mike Selvaggio	Malcolm Gladwell	Jeff Wu
Ed Hatch	Ken Blanchard	Abraham Lincoln
Jackie Leavenworth	John C Maxwell	Frank Serio
Rich Sands	Harvey Mackay	Morgan Jones

Robert Morris	Victor Frankl	Gail Ailor
Lee Barrett	Keith Ferrazzi	Jo Mangum
Joel Osteen	Ivan Misner	Chris Cooper
Jason Donahey	John Assaraf	Ted Williams
Katrina Donahey	Stephen Covey	Jack White
Dale Carnegie	Harry Beckwith	Tower of Power
James Allen	Simon Sinek	Brendon Burchard

You can reach me at:

Mark Given International
P.O. Box 1460
Roanoke Rapids, NC 27870

252-536-1169
mark@markgiven.com
http://www.markgiven.com

You might also consider making the world a little better by sharing this book with someone else. If you choose to not give it away, please know that you can purchase as many extra copies as you want or need!

21860581R00085